Literary IRELAND

TOM KELLY
Photographs

PETER SOMERVILLE-LARGE
Text

ROBERTS RINEHART PUBLISHERS
Boulder, Colorado
Dublin, Ireland

To Val

Published by ROBERTS RINEHART PUBLISHERS

6309 Monarch Park Place, Niwot, Colorado 80503

Tel 303.652.2685   Fax 303.652.2689

www.robertsrinehart.com

Distributed to the trade in the U.S. and Canada by
Publishers Group West

Published in Ireland and the UK by
Roberts Rinehart Publishers
Trinity House, Charleston Road, Dublin 6, Ireland

International Standard Book Number 1-57098-230-9

Library of Congress Catalog Card Number 97-69449

Printed in China

Design: Jack Van Zandt and Ann W. Douden

PHOTOGRAPHS

TITLE PAGE: *Connemara*

THIS PAGE: *West Cork*

FOLLOWING PAGE: *Carrowmore, County Sligo*

The quote on page 128 is taken from the poem
"Under Ben Bulben" by W. B. Yeats.

Contents

Antiquity 7

The Pale and Beyond 25

Tír na nÓg 53

The Dubliners 87

The Widening Gyre 111

A Sense of Place 131

Biographies 154

Antiquity

Easkey, County Sligo

Summer dries up the stream
Swift cattle search for water
Heather spreads its hair
The white bog cotton blooms.

An anonymous eighth-century poet incorporates a hymn to summer in an account of the boyhood deeds of Finn MacCumhaill. His contemporary writes of the coming of winter, a time of fear:

Bog Cotton

Sliabh Cua, dark and broken, is full of wolf packs
The wind sweeps down its glens,
wolves howl about its dykes,
the fierce dark deer bellows
across it in the Autumn,
and the crane cries out across its rocks.

Connemara

Connemara

Connemara

Beara, County Cork

Unexcavated mound, County Tipperary

Surviving Irish texts show how landscape dominated prose and poetry from the beginning. Settings for religious poetry were among forests, trees, mountains, singing birds, and bellowing deer. The seas offered their terrors. In myth, where the forest was cleared, there emerged the sites of battlefields. Literary landmarks spreading through time reach to Coole, the hills above Glencar, Shancoduff, and the briar-edged hayfields in County Derry where the boy Heaney picked blackberries fat with "summer's blood."

Before the Christian era the plains of Meath, the table mountain of Knocknarea, the shores of Derryvaragh and the plateau above the sea of Moyle off County Antrim were among those hundreds of majestic locations where Cuchulainn, the Children of Lir and other legendary protagonists played their part in epic literature. In County Roscommon, at Rathangan, the seat of the kings in Connaught, from where

County Cavan

Queen Maeve set off to steal the Brown Bull of Cooley, there are still scores of lumpy unexcavated traces of the past. They were there when the poet wrote in the *Leabhar na hUidhre*, the Book of the Brown Cow:

There are fifty mounds in the hall of Cruacha,
Fifty brave worthy men
Are beneath these mounds.

Ancient kings, Bruide, Cathal, Aedh, and Mael Duin, are remembered in a sixth-century verse whose subject is a rath in an oak wood in County Kildare. "The rath survives; the kings are covered in clay." By then the time had come when heroes had to share the songs of scribes and poets with saints and holy men. With the coming of Christianity natural observation played a meticulous part in praise for God's creation.

County Meath

The tradition of monastic poems, most of them anonymous, is linked to the age of hermits. Throughout Europe in the early middle ages the forest had become a place for penitents, a substitute for the wilderness in Egypt or Sinai to which the early fathers had fled. In Ireland lonely monks sat in "humble hidden" huts with ivy roofs in the "path filled" forest eating dry bread and drinking clear water. Penitence became linked with delight. In their retreats they paid tribute to the Creator as they sat looking at the sunlight on the margin of their missals or listened to pigeons or the blackbird in the gorse beside Belfast Lough.

Perhaps the best known of these poems that praise the monastic life is the exchange between King Guaire, a seventh-century king of Connaught, and the hermit Marban, his half-brother, whose "hut in the wood" has been located by clues in the poem to east Galway. Marban not only details his surroundings, the

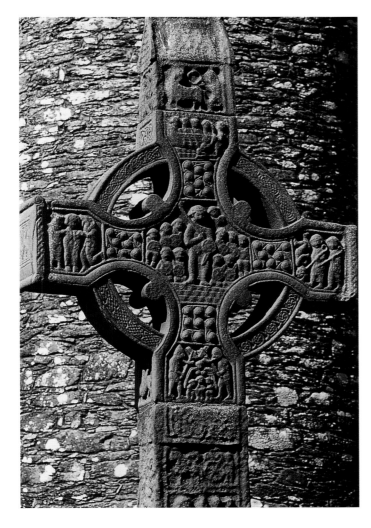

Monasterboice, County Louth

forest oaks and yews, the rowans and hazels whose nuts contribute to his simple diet, but also the wild creatures that surround him—the stags, foxes, wild pigs, wild geese, birds, and humming insects. He does not dwell on the problems of winter. Instead, the summer scene provokes a cry of envy from King Guaire, who declares that he would give up his kingdom if he could be with his brother.

The forest with its yew, holly, birch, and aspen is the refuge of Sweeney, who is reputed to have been driven mad during the battle of Mag Rath in the seventh century. In verses which have been translated and interpreted by many poets, Sweeney names the places he roams, from the Mourne Mountains to the Slieve Aughty in County Clare, to Kerry, to the Liffey valley, and the Knockmealdowns. All Ireland, and a bit of Scotland, including Ailsa Craig, is encapsulated in Sweeney's frenzies before he foretells his death where the tide changes at St. Mullins on the Barrow river in County Carlow.

Over the centuries most of the forest which provided refuge for the monks and a passage for Sweeney's journeys has disappeared. The destruction of forest was taking place throughout Europe, but in Ireland it became associated with conquest as the invaders cut down ancient trees for charcoal and ship spars. The lament for Kilcash, the old Catholic castle on the slopes of Slievenamon, written in the eighteenth century, perhaps by a priest, Father Lane, mourned the passing of the gracious old ways, with the felling of the trees and the passing of the birds.

> *No cuckoo on top of the boughs there,*
> *Singing the world to rest.*

Over a century later, Lord Cloncurry's daughter, Emily Lawless, wrote similarly in her "Dirge of the Munster Forest":

> *The axe is sharpened to cut down my pride*
> *I pass, I die and leave no natural heirs . . .*

There are still a few forested places that recall the rhapsodies of Marban. Arboreal survivors include the oak woods of Kerry or the stretch of trees at Shillaleagh recently saved from the sharpened axe. Those that have literary associations include the woods in Sligo and the seven woods of Coole, tended by Lady Gregory.

Timahoe Tower, County Laois

County Laois

Glendalough, County Wicklow

Above: County Meath   *Following page: County Carlow*

The Pale
and Beyond

County Kerry

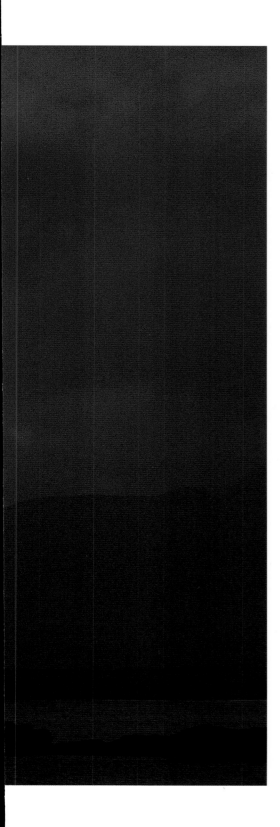

$\mathcal{W}$ith the coming of the Normans arrived Gerald of Wales, whose *Topographia*, published in 1188, was used for centuries as a reliable guide to Ireland. "There is . . . such a plentiful supply of rain," he wrote with some truth, "such an ever-present overhanging of clouds and fog, that you will scarcely see even in the summer consecutive days of really fine weather." From Giraldus's time foreign travellers have their place in the landscape of literature. They skip through the centuries, complaining about the weather, and local customs, always commenting on Irish hospitality. They observed the countryside with sharp strangers' eyes. They include Fynes Moryson, who was in Ireland at the end of the sixteenth century; Sir William Brereton, a few decades after, enjoying "very free and courteous entertainment" during his travels in Wexford; the French aristocrat Chevalier de la Tocayne leaping into the Shannon at its mouth to take a swim; and Thomas Carlyle, whose vivid staccato gives the impression of being written jerkily as he was borne along in a carriage:

> Donegal mountains, blue-black over Donegal Bay . . . moory raggedness with green patches near, all treeless . . . nothing distinct till narrow street of Ballyshannon, mills, breweries, considerable confused much-whitewashed country town.

Ballyshannon, County Donegal

Atlantic Coast, County Donegal

Lough Arrow, Carrowkeel, County Sligo

Midlands rainbows

Lough Gill, County Kerry

*T*ravelers' tales have a special place in the literary landscape, precisely because so much of their interest is topographical observation. Of those who stayed, one of those most influenced by details of the Irish scene was Edmund Spenser. In 1589 Spenser received from the English Crown just over three thousand acres in north Cork which included the castle of Kilcolman. Here in "savage soil, far from Parnasso's Mount" he blended the landmarks around his estates, the Ballyhoura hills, and the river running near his castle, the "sweet Awbeg", into *The Fairie Queene* and *Colin Clout's Come Home Again*. His propagandist *A View of the Present State of Ireland* has a passage revealing his love for the Irish landscape:

> Sure it is . . . a most beautiful and sweet country as any is under heaven: seamed throughout with many goodly rivers, replenished with all sorts of fish, most abundantly sprinkled with many sweet islands and goodly lakes, like little inland seas . . . adorned with goodly woods fit for building of . . . ships, so commodiously, as that if some princes in the world had them, they would soon hope to be lords of all the seas, and ere long of all the world . . .

For many years the bardic tradition survived in the face of invasion. Noble Irish families maintained hereditary poets whose forte was paeons of praise, like the panegyric on Thomas Butler by Flann McGrath which dwelt on details of the gabled house in Carrick-on-Suir with sunlight streaming through its mullioned windows. But after the Battle of Kinsale, 1601, Irish poetry reflected the preoccupations of a subject people. Many of the themes of the displaced bards, some of whom found new patrons among the Anglo-Irish, were bitter or nostalgic.

After the failure of the Jacobite cause one popular form of Gaelic poetry was the *aisling*, in which the poet encounters a woman who is a visionary foretelling the revival of Stuart fortunes. At the end of the eighteenth century Brian Merriman, Clare schoolmaster, illegitimate son of a country gentleman, wrote his notorious parody of the *aisling* convention. *Cúirt an Mhéan Oíche* (*The Midnight Court*) is a one-thousand-line comic and bawdy burlesque of bardic pretensions. But it also contains a tender passage of natural description of the Clare countryside on a summer morning. In the early stanzas the poet is walking beside a river, catching sight of Lough Gréine, and the mountains behind, his heart lightening at the sight of shoals of ducks, a swan, fishes jumping in the sun, and the birds in the trees.

River Boyne, County Meath

At the time Merriman was writing his masterpiece, Dublin was developing, in the words of Louis MacNeice, from the Fort of the Dane, garrison of the Saxon, towards its apogee as the Augustan capital of a Gaelic nation. (No one better than MacNeice for townscapes: Belfast "between the mountains and the gantries," Carrickfergus "where the bottle-neck harbour collects the mud which jams the little boats beneath the Norman castle.") In 1714 Jonathan Swift, one of the capital's greatest citizens, returned to live as Dean "in wretched Dublin in miserable Ireland." But he became a champion of the country where he found himself. He understood the English view of Ireland, and propounded it in his fourth Drapier letter:

> As to *Ireland* they know little more than they do of *Mexico*; further than that it is a Country subject to the King of England full of Boggs, inhabited by wild *Irish Papists*; . . . And their general Opinion is, that it were better for *England* if this whole Island were sunk into the Sea . . .

There are bucolic touches in Swift's writing, like his comparison of the farmer's goose and the poet in "The Progress of Poetry." But generally he is not remembered for his appreciation of landscape; the best known of his natural descriptions may be his Latin poem, "Rupes Carberiae" (The Rocks of Carbury), composed on a visit to West Cork. However, he had a passion for gardening. He planted trees and made a fish pond at Laracor. He wrote, in imitation of Horace:

> *I often wish'd that I had clear*
> *For Life six hundred Pounds a Year*
> *A handsome House to lodge a Friend*
> *A River at my Garden's End,*
> *A Terras Walk and half a Rood*
> *Of Land set out to plant a Wood.*

In 1721 he acquired a plot of land beside St. Patrick's Cathedral which typically he named Naboth's Vineyard. The garden he created with its crops of peaches, nectarines, pears and paradise apples, its roses and gravel walks and "rustling . . . trees," had a river walk, "winding and meandering" beside the Poddle, and an open view towards the Wicklow Hills.

Swift's enthusiasm was typical of an Anglo-Irish obsession, an urge to create an ordered landscape within the demesne—a word derived from *dominicus*, meaning the lord's house. Henceforth the garden and the pleasure grounds appear in Anglo-Irish literature either as symbols of the defensive *hortus enclosus*, or used as subtle indica tors of social status, or in simple descriptive passages written by those still following the old bardic tradition. There are many examples of this sort of verse:

Durrow, County Offaly

. . . the groves and the meadow charming
The pleasant gardens of Castle Hyde

or

My humble muse awake and sing the praise
Of lovely Glin in simple artless lays . . .

or

Oh Newcourt is the prettiest place in Carbury
I ween,
Environed by great grandeur, and pine-groves
ever green.
It also is an ancient place of fame and high
renown,
Prettily situated, and convenient to the town.

The landscape of the big house was to take a more sophisticated place in literature in the novels of Maria Edgeworth like *The Absentee* where the garden and demesne reflect the attitudes and action of her personifications—the nouveau riche, the good agent, or the improvident landlord. A century later Somerville and Ross brilliantly expressed the social nuances of gardening in their masterpiece, *The Real Charlotte*.

Edith Somerville and Violet Martin, writing as Somerville and Ross, placed the action of *The Real Charlotte* in the Galway where Martin was brought up, evoking Ross House beside Lough Corrib. Their other novels never came near the towering achievement of this masterpiece. They found more fame and money in their anecdotes about the resident magistrate, prolonging their *Irish R.M.* stories to three volumes. The unfortunate R.M. lives in West Cork, and his misadventures take place in the landscape around Edith Somerville's home in Castletownsend. In Patrick Kavanagh's phrase, "the ditches and lanes come alive" in Somerville and Ross. Amid the humor the country and the sea are described with a vividness arising from familiarity and love, whether the protagonists are shooting woodcock, sea voyaging, as in "The House of Fahy" where the pleasure yacht makes a nightmare voyage into Bantry Bay, or hunting.

County Meath

Bantry Bay, County Cork

County Kerry

The literature of hunting goes back to the Fianna. In the eighteenth century, songs which involved the fox and red hunting coats were popular with Hellfire Clubs and convivial gatherings after a good day out after Reynard. Songs like the Kilruddery Hunt take in the landscape of South Dublin with the rhythm of a galloping horse as the fox makes his way "To Carrickmines thence, and to Cherriwood then, Steep Shankhill he clim'd and to Ballyman Glen."

In the nineteenth century Charles O'Malley and W. H. Maxwell wrote about hunting in the west. In this century Molly Keane was as active a huntswoman as Somerville and Ross. Like them she was an amateur horse coper, which was considered a respectable occupation for impoverished gentlewomen, and her love and knowledge of horseflesh permeates her novels.

More recently Molly Keane took a purring pleasure in describing the surroundings of houses where her characters are tearing each other to pieces. There are few better writers to evoke the expensive scents of carefully nurtured flowers, the parma violets, the verbena and the winter hazel which people are forever sniffing if they are not out on their horses. Occasionally her writing sounds like a garden catalogue:

There you went up and down half-circular flights of steps and breathed the hushed air in grassy spaces. You walked among towering rhododendrons, . . . and saw the air blue in the bamboos and eucalyptus and golden in the sticky apricot of azaleas . . .

Fox hunting, County Laois

Another Anglo-Irish woman whose work was saturated with the atmosphere of the place where she was reared is Elizabeth Bowen. North Cork and her own family house, Bowenscourt, appear in novels like the elegiac *The Last September* where a house is doomed to be burnt during the Troubles. When she wrote her loving history of her home, Bowen's Court, there was a sense of foreboding about her detailed description as if she knew that soon it would only survive on paper. It is the presentiment of doom conveyed in Yeats' poem about Coole.

George Moore's great semi-autobiography, *Hail and Farewell*, in which he recalls his boyhood at Moore Hall beside Lough Carra, has no rival in its description of the life and landscape of the Big House. Outside the demesne he uses the pathetic fallacy that nature sympathizes with our feelings in combining the weeping landscapes of Mayo with human unhappiness, "the blank snow-laden country, with its sepulchral mountains disappearing in the grey masses of cloud that the evening, like winding-sheets, slowly and silently unrolled . . . "

The Big House would arouse fury, not only from the dispossessed poets of the eighteenth century. There is no Yeatsean regret when contemporary poet Michael Hartnett turns his wrath on Castletown—when, absorbing its graceful beauty, he sees "black figures dancing on the lawn, *Eviction, Droit de Seigneur, Broken Bones* . . . "

Mullaghmore, County Sligo

Conaghra, County Mayo

Inevitably, given Irish history, the landscape of ruin has a parallel place in literature. Oliver Goldsmith spent an idyllic childhood in County Longford; he modeled the family of *The Vicar of Wakefield* on his own. The Rev. Charles Goldsmith loved children who followed him "with endearing wile." He would be seen on summer evenings on the Athlone-Ballymahon road leading a black pony (Blackberry in *The Vicar of Wakefield*) yoked to a trap full of children enjoying a free ride. But youthful happiness is illusory and the poet chose to remember his birthplace, Lissoy, disguised as a location in England, as the deserted village, ruined by Ireland's harsh history:

> *No more the glassy brook reflects the day,*
> *But chok'd with sedges works its weedy way*
> *. . . Amidst thy desert walks the lapwing flies*
> *And tires their echoes with unvaried cries.*
> *Sunk are thy bowers in shapeless ruin all . . .*

Desolation both romantic and fashionable was a feature of Lady Morgan's forgotten *Florence Macarthy*:

> Two lodges mouldered on either side into absolute ruin, and the . . . Grecian portico . . . was . . . obvious in the scattered fragments of friezes and entablatures which lay choked amidst heaps of nettles, furze-bushes and long rye-grass . . .

Ruin was also Thomas Rolleston's theme, best remembered for "Clonmacnoise," his treatment of a lament from the Irish of Angus O'Gillan:

> *In a quiet water'd land, a land of roses,*
> *Stands Saint Kieran's city fair . . .*

The sight of a wrecked house set Anthony Trollope writing novels. "Oh what a picture of misery, of useless expenditure, and premature decay." The ivy-covered ruin near Brosna, County Leitrim, is still to be seen. A century and a half later, decay preoccupies the poet Derek Mahon whose "A Disused Shed in Co. Wexford" suggests nightmares of history with its "grim dominion of stale air and rank moisture."

Yeats summed up the Anglo-Irish dilemma in "The Curse of Cromwell" with the old ruin that the winds howled through. He was prophetic in writing the destruction of Coole. Lady Gregory also knew that her house was doomed, although she kept it going until her death. In 1924 that sturdy old gardener and lover of trees drove from Coole to her family home, Roxborough, recently burnt in the troubles,

> just the walls standing, blackened, and all the long yards silent . . . The garden is grass and weeds but some phloxes that Kathie had planted are not yet choked and I am bringing them here, a great enrichment to my borders.

County Laois

Rosserk Friary, County Mayo

Tír na nÓg

Atlantic Coast, County Clare

$\mathcal{L}$ady Gregory's work in compiling and popularizing folklore was a contributing factor to the Gaelic revival. In the early nineteenth century the poetry of lament was continued in the ballads of Thomas Davis and J. J. Callanan and James Clarence Mangan, who worked from ancient Gaelic sources. Then writers and compilers like Lady Gregory and Douglas Hyde helped to bring Gaelic to the patriotic masses. As a result, hundreds of enthusiasts traveled to the west of Ireland where Irish was still spoken and the shorelines were wild and beautiful. A typical visitor to Inishmaan in the Aran Islands was Kathleen Sheehy, the mother of Conor Cruise O'Brien. Her conversation is attributed by James Joyce in his story "The Dead" to Miss Ivors when she accuses Gabriel Conroy of being a West Briton when he shows more interest in the continent than in Ireland's wild west.

$\mathcal{A}$nother visitor to the Aran Islands, John Millington Synge, journeyed to Inishmore in the summer of 1898.

> Here and there a band of tall girls passed me on their way to Kilronan and called out to me . . . speaking English with a slight foreign intonation . . . The rain and cold seemed to have no influence on their vitality, and as they hurried past me with eager laughter and great talking in Gaelic, they left the wet masses of rock more desolate then before.

> Pegeen Mike in Synge's famous *The Playboy of the Western World* may well have been among them, "a wild-looking but fine girl of about twenty."

Although Synge's wanderings in the west of Ireland and in Wicklow provided the material for his drama, the settings of his plays do not encompass much landscape. *The Well of the Saints* and *The Tinker's Wedding* are both set by roadsides, the last one "after nightfall." The action of his other dramas is indoors. We learn that *In the Shadow of the Glen* takes place in "the last cottage at the head of a long glen in County Wicklow"—a prison from which the Tramp offers to release her:

Come along with me now, lady of the house, and . . . you'll be hearing the herons crying out over the black lakes, and you'll be hearing the grouse and the owls with them, and the larks and the big thrushes when the day is warm.

The shebeen "very rough and untidy" "on a wild coast of Mayo" where the playboy Christy Mahon tells his tall tale has a "door into the open air" at the back, a little to the left of the counter—the sun shines in during Act Two, and the crowd surges in and out from the sands outside as the action in *The Playboy of the Western World* reaches its climax. On the island off the west of Ireland where *Riders to the Sea* is located, the audience has no visual clues to the lethal power of the sea and the echoes of the calm after the storm outside, apart from "some new boards" standing in the cottage kitchen. "Bartley will have a fine coffin out of the white boards, and a deep grave surely. What more can we want than that? No man can be living forever and we must be satisfied."

Illannonearaun, County Clare

County Kerry

The Cliffs of Moher, County Clare

The Cliffs of Moher, County Clare

West Cork

Achill Island, County Mayo

Clare Island, Clew Bay, County Mayo

The Blasket Islands, County Kerry

Island people created their own literature. The Gaelic revival sent scholars to the west seeking the purest sources of the language. Those who came to the Blasket Islands (off the southwest coast of Kerry) to be taught Irish by local farmer-fishermen included the Englishman Robin Flower, and Brian O Ceallaigh. As a result of their interest, among the people of the Blaskets a number of people were encouraged to write accounts of their lives. Tomás O Criomhthain, born in 1856 on the Great Blasket, wrote *An tOileánach*, later translated into English as *The Islandman*. When it was published in 1929 it was immediately recognized as a major event in modern Irish literature.

Muiris O Súilleabháin's *Fiche Blian ag Fás* was an exercise in nostalgia written after he had left the Great Blasket and gone to live in Connemara

Dingle and the Blasket Islands, County Kerry

as a Civic Guard. Translated as *Twenty Years a-Growing*, it is the best known of the island autobiographies, although many purists prefer the tough spare narrative of Tomás O Criomhthain. Peig Sayers, born in 1873, who was known on the Blaskets as the Queen of the Storytellers, wrote classic accounts of island life in *Peig*, and *Machtnamh Sean-Mhná*, translated as *An Old Woman's Reflections*.

These three authors, together with others who spent part of their lives on the Blaskets, record the harsh yet rewarding routines of the farmer-fishermen who snatched their living from the sea and from their small holdings. Life was a constant battle for survival. Of Tomás O Criomhthain's ten children, one fell over a cliff, another drowned "trying to save the lady off the White Strand," while others died of disease.

Lettermore Island, County Galway

The cottages, with their perpetual turf fires, the animals inside, (the calf "with the run of the kitchen or lying muzzle to the fire") and the hens in the thatch, were built against a stupendous background—the seascape that included the other islands Inishnabró and Inishvickillane with their seals and seabirds and rabbits, Tearaght, the western Island made distinct by its lighthouse, and the northern island Tooskert, rising above cliffs.

The narrators combine acute observation of their limited but changeable surroundings, and wit in their account of the struggle for existence, the battles with the elements, and the pleasures of close companionship. They lived on the edge of the Atlantic and shared the struggles of the seals and birds, whose eggs they stole to eat, guillemots, seagulls and razor-bills. In one extraordinary episode Tomás O Criomhthain and his companions row close enough to a whale to experience its halitosis. It is not altogether surprising that Flann O'Brien, writing as Myles na Gopeleen, chose to satirize the genre, condemning Robin Flower's overblown translations, in his savagely funny parody *An Béal Bocht*, which means *The Poor Mouth*.

Turf bank, Connemara

Peat bog, Connemara

Deserted village, Achill Island, County Mayo

Burren, County Clare

Connemara

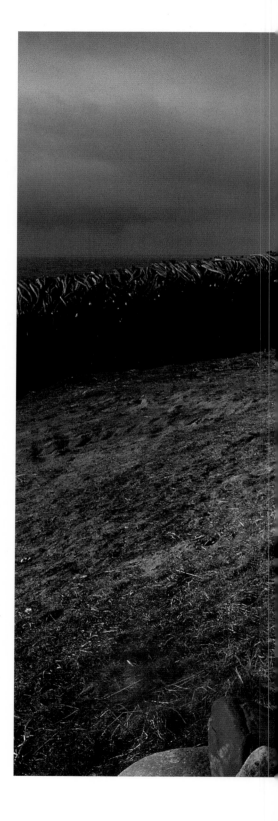

Seaweed and stones, Connemara

Doogort, Achill Island, County Mayo

Doolin, County Clare

County Mayo

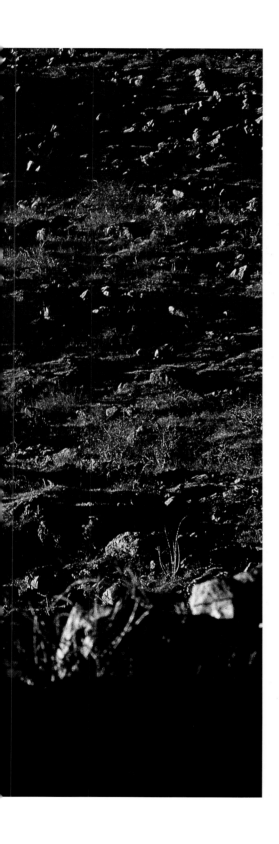

County Mayo

The Aran Islands had literary traditions also. One poet of distinction, Máirtín O Direáin, came from the Aran Islands; Liam O'Flaherty also was born on Inishmore in 1897 and brought up in an Irish-speaking community. The clever boy was lifted to the mainland, and educated with the notion that he should become a priest. However he had no vocation, and after a spell in the British army, which made him deeply unpopular among his own people, he took part in the Troubles and the Civil War. In 1923 he wrote his first novel, *Thy Neighbour's Wife*, set in the Aran Islands. *Skerrett*, a later novel, concerned an island feud between priest and schoolmaster. O'Flaherty may be best known for his searing novella *The Informer*, but his reputation rests mostly on his short stories, imbued with country backgrounds. Many are concerned with Aran, like "Timoney's Ass," a wry hymn to freedom where the animal celebrates his escape to an island's rocky wilderness with a harsh triumphant braying.

$\mathcal{L}$ike O'Flaherty, Frank O'Connor and Seán O'Faoláin were caught in the Troubles and the Civil War. Both these writers were from Cork. They used the background of West Cork for their most effective stories of the period: the patch of bog that is the scene of the ghastly climax of O'Connor's "Guests of the Nation" or the hinterland of Inchigeela through which the Irregulars flee in O'Faoláin's "The Patriot." O'Faoláin's stories ranged from Dublin to Donegal, Mayo, and Limerick, but for all the variety of his experience, it is in his native Cork that his writing is most vivid. The haunting "The Silence of the Valley," set in Gougane Barra, is a tribute to Timothy Buckeley, the persecuted tailor who died in 1944 and whose funeral and wake, described by O'Faoláin, were attended by many who admired him. The tailor's personality had been lovingly depicted by Eric Cross in *The Tailor and Ansty*, published and banned in 1942 for reasons that are incomprehensible today.

Bog and reeds

Bog

Right: West Cork
Following page: Galway Bay

The Dubliners

Dublin skyline

In the nation's capital, a unique literary cityscape evolved over the early years of the twentieth century. While pioneering the modern short story in a way so radical that he had great difficulty in finding a publisher for his collection *Dubliners*, James Joyce embarked on his eighteen hours of Dublin experience. His boast that Dublin could be rebuilt from the pages of *Ulysses* was an absurd one. He ignored the city's great buildings (apart from the National Library) and its Georgian heritage except when they occurred incidentally—the converted drawing-room which is the labor ward at Holles Street hospital or the broken fanlights of Monto that make up the fronts of the whorehouses.

But the topography of *Ulysses* takes in a good deal of the Dublin of 1904; both Leopold Bloom and Stephen Daedalus may have been joggers to cover so large an area. The only time Bloom takes a rest as he travels is in the cab that takes him out to Paddy Dignan's funeral at Glasnevin. Stephen has a lot of walking to do as he makes his way into the city from the Martello Tower at Sandycove to Sandymount Strand on the wrinkled sand below Leahy's Terrace. From Bloom's house in Eccles Street (another good Georgian house, but with a singularly unprepossessing interior) to the cabman's shelter run by the informer, Skin-the-Goat, Joyce recreated his own Dublin with the aid of newspaper cuttings and memory capable of total recall.

Crossing the Liffey

Early morning

Windmill Lane

Joyce's contemporary Sean O'Casey constructed another Dublin, not only in his plays, but in his sparkling, exhilarating, infuriating, inaccurate (O'Casey was a man for the adjectives) autobiographies. Like many a good book, the first volume, *I Knock at the Door,* was banned. He recounts his Dublin experiences from the 1880s when young Sean (known in his Protestant family as Johnny) slips into a world of horses and soldiers and dying slum children. His story stretches from his efforts to become a patriot with the aid of O'Growney's *Simple Lessons in Irish* while working as a laborer with the Great Northern Railway, to his departure for England after the rejection of *The Silver Tassie.*

He did not begin to write the autobiographies until 1939. Sixteen years previously his *The Shadow of a Gunman* announced a new major talent on the Irish stage (and incidentally helped the Abbey Theatre out of near bankruptcy). In this and his subsequent tragi-comedies *The Plough and the Stars* and *Juno and the Paycock*, set against a background of tenement life, he exposed the false promises and tragedies of patriotism in dilemmas that are still relevant.

The Dublin of Brendan Behan is somber. His prison experiences in Mountjoy jail in the early 1940s (he was serving a sentence for shooting a policeman) gave him material for *The Quare Fellow*, first performed in 1954. His other major play, *The Hostage*, owed much to Frank O'Connor's powerful *Guests of the Nation*; by that time O'Connor was used to his story being adapted and copied by other authors. Behan died aged forty-one in 1963 after sad years of self-destructive behavior witnessed by many a Dublin pub-goer. The slender body of work that he left behind, including his fine autobiography *Borstal Boy*, inspires a lasting regret that he did not have the time or temperament to achieve more.

Mountjoy Square

Cityscape from atop the Guinness Brewery

Temple Bar

Homage to Beckett

Merrion Square

*F*lann O'Brien grew up in Herbert Place on a stretch of canal further east to the watery place at Baggot Street remembered by poet Patrick Kavanagh; here is the setting for some of the eccentricities of O'Brien's *The Hard Life*. *At-Swim-Two-Birds* owes a good deal to Avoca Avenue in Blackrock, while Dalkey took on a weird new atmosphere in *The Dalkey Archive*. In *Malone Dies* Beckett also used this comfortable south county suburb as a background where a boatload of lunatics is ferried out to Dalkey Island.

Seamus O'Sullivan wrote about the shabby little room in Nelson Street with the bronze tea-pot and the singing bird; elsewhere he described the lamplighter leaving "faint blue bubbles in his wake" and the funeral cabs processing to Glasnevin cemetery.

Stately, sombre, stepping slow
The white-plumed funeral horses go . . .

Dublin Bay

Phoenix Park

It may be no coincidence that the dark streets of Dublin with lamplight and gaslight causing flickering shadows on decayed houses aroused the imaginations of three writers of horror during the nineteenth century. Charles Robert Maturin's *Melmoth the Wanderer* was a milestone in Gothic horror; after his disgrace Oscar Wilde took the name of the outcast Melmoth. Sipping green tea, Sheridan Le Fanu gazed out of the drawing-room window of his house in Merrion Square, imagining the terrors of *Uncle Silas*, or the fat moist white hand speeding up the curtain in *The House by the Churchyard* at Chapelizod. Bram Stoker never visited Transylvania before he wrote the tale of Count Dracula but only read a guidebook. Perhaps some nightmare dreamed in Clontarf turned into the most enduring image of horror of the twentieth century.

Waiting for Godot

There is horror in the settings of Samuel Beckett's plays with their minimal landscapes. Groping for a "literature of the unword," he had no time for realism, and the plays need no more than the country road, the tree, perhaps a willow, perhaps a shrub, and the mound where Estragon pulls at his boot in *Waiting for Godot*. Or the expanse of scorched earth, the unbroken plain and sky and the other mound in which Winnie, the well-preserved blonde in *Happy Days,* is embedded (initially) up to her waist. But his short stories *More Pricks than Kicks* are full of Dublin and the claustrophobic atmosphere of Carrickmines with its view of the mountains and the slow and easy train to Harcourt Street.

County Cork

Mullaghveal, County Kerry

The
Widening
Gyre

*W*illiam Butler Yeats lived the first three years of his life in Sandymount, then a respectable suburb of Dublin, before his family moved to London where he spent his boyhood. But he went for his holidays to the house of his grandfather, William Pollexfen, in Sligo, the harbor set between Knocknarea and Ben Bulben like a nut caught in nutcrackers. Over his lifetime many great themes blended into Yeats's poetry—love, politics, mythology, theater, the Orient, spiritualism and mysticism, but from the earliest times after he decided that he would be a poet, the landscape of those summers fixes his poetry in Sligo:

> *. . . in boyhood when with rod and fly*
> *Or the humbler worm, I climbed Ben Bulben's back*
> *And had the livelong summer day to spend.*

Fishing, Lough Nafooey, Galway/Mayo border

Benbo Mountains, County Sligo

County Sligo

Northwest County Mayo

The best known of his early poems encompass similar moments of his youth, like "The Stolen Child" where a fairy spirit lures a child away to various beauty spots in the Sligo area. In his stupendous late poetry he could escape from "the foul rag-and-bone shop of the heart" to create the stormy images of the country he had known:

There in the tomb stand the dead upright
But winds come up from the shore:
They shake when the winds roar,
Old bones upon the mountain shake.

Mountains, lakes, rivers, the Big House Lissadell with its great windows opening to the south, and the busy little seaport of Sligo are interwoven into his lyrics, together with the sea and the seashore:

. . . Cuchulain stirred,
Stared on the horses of the sea, and heard
The cars of battle and his own name cried;
And fought with the invulnerable tide.

County Galway

Lough Gill, County Sligo

The Burren, County Clare

Lough Ennell, County Westmeath

In middle age his friendship with Lady Gregory brought him to East Galway and to Coole Park, another Big House surrounded by woodland:

I have heard the pigeons of the Seven Woods
Make their faint thunder . . .

Nearby was the lake where on an autumn evening he counted fifty-nine swans. The swans, the hawk, the squirrel at Kyle-na-no have their place in his poems with the fairies dancing on the sands at the Rosses.

A few miles from Coole Park was a sixteenth-century tower house, Thoor Ballylee. Here Yeats spent a number of summers writing great verse where his surroundings are a background for his contemplation on war and violence and "phantoms of hatred." In his meditations he describes his surroundings in detail, the tower beside the bridge, the elms, thorn trees, the river with its splashing cows and water-hen and chicks. The stare's nest (a stare is a starling) by his window to which he invites the honey-bees becomes a metaphor for renewal after the heart has "grown brutal."

But it was to Sligo he returned in his final poem with its "command" for a limestone headstone cut with a simple epitaph.

Knocknarea, County Sligo

County Sligo

Irish poets, learn your trade
Sing whatever is well made,
Scorn the sort now growing up
All out of shape from toe to top
Their unremembering hearts and heads
Base-born products of base beds.
Sing the peasantry, and then
Hard-riding country gentlemen,
The holiness of monks, and after
Porter-drinkers' randy laughter;
Sing the lords and ladies gay
That were beaten into clay
Through seven heroic centuries;
Cast your mind on other days
That we in coming days may be
Still the indomitable Irishry.

Under bare Ben Bulben's head
In Drumcliff churchyard Yeats is laid,
An ancestor was rector there
Long years ago; a church stands near,
By the road an ancient Cross.
No marble, no conventional phrase,
On limestone quarried near the spot
By his command these words be cut:

Cast a cold eye
On life, on death.
Horseman, pass by!

A Sense of Place

Previous page: West Kerry

Above: County Meath

he variety of landscapes compressed into so small an island has encouraged a geographic lyricism where few places are omitted, and each is distinct as the style of those who make it their own. Ireland has been mapped out by her writers in a patchwork of poetry and prose. "That's his place" we are proud to point out, and in Feakle or Monaghan or Sligo or West Wicklow fame is marked by the creation of a summer school.

In Meath Lord Dunsany wrote an immense amount in his great castle. But today he is chiefly remembered for encouraging Mary Lavin, who took over the stretch of land near Bective with its ancient abbey and placed it on the literary map, and for discovering Francis Ledwidge. In his short life Ledwidge wrote a number of nature poems like "A Twilight in Middle March."

River Boyne, County Meath

Within the oak a throb of pigeon wings
Fell silent and grey twilight hushed the fold,
And spiders' hammocks swung on half-ope'd things
That shook like foreigners upon our cold

A gipsy made a fire and made a sound
Of moving tins, and from an oblong moon
The river seemed to gush across the ground
To the cracked metre of a marching tune.

County Meath

F. R. Higgins also had Meath in mind when he wrote of a summer's day:

Here, drowned within their dewy deeps of June
The fields, for graziers, gather every silver;
And while each isle becomes a bush in time
The Boyne flows into airy stillness.

Patrick Kavanagh's Monaghan—Mullahinsha, Drummeril, Black Shanco—is a rougher terrain.

O stony grey soil of Monaghan,
You sang on the steamy dung-hills
A song of the coward's brood
You perfumed my clothes with weasel itch
You fed me on swinish food . . .

The spare weary beauty of John McGahern's prose is filled with detail of the watery places of Leitrim and Roscommon that seldom softens the misery of his characters—the stutter of the kingfisher, the watercress, whitethorn, and bullrushes of the lakes and the Shannon river.

Lough Key, County Roscommon

Brandon, County Kerry

In *The Country Girls*, Edna O'Brien remembered her home near Feakle beside a more southern stretch of the Shannon not far from where Merriman found his Midnight Court. In her description of a spring morning O'Brien writes of

. . . the fields very green and very peaceful. Outside the paling wire was a walnut tree and under its shade there were bluebells, tall and intensely blue, a grotto of heaven-blue flowers among the limestone boulders. And my swing was swaying in the wind, and all the leaves on all the tree-tops were stirring lightly.

The landscapes of north Kerry and the wild reaches of Limerick are the settings for the work of Bryan MacMahon and John B. Keane, both of

County Limerick

whom were born in Listowel. MacMahon's collections of short stories, including *The Lion Tamer* and *The Sound of Hooves,* rank with the best of Irish writing. John B. Keane's plays, including *Sive, The Year of the Hiker* and *Big Maggie*, are idiosyncratic, their source often derived from local stories and personalities whose behavior tends to be passionate, even lurid. These plays, threaded with Kerry humor, have proved immensely popular with playgoers, in spite of having been largely ignored by critics. His work reached an international public when *The Field*, containing elements of a real-life melodrama, was made into a film. Keane's short stories and novels draw deeply from his natural environs. John B. Keane continues to write in Listowel where he keeps a public house, the perfect base for seeking out his material.

West Cork

County Kerry

illiam Trevor grew up in rural Cork, spending his childhood in three towns where his father was bank manager: Youghal, Mitchelstown ,and Skibbereen. His school days in the Dublin mountains have also infiltrated his work. But it is the atmosphere of County Cork in the 1930s and 1940s that he remembers with obsessive detail. His best-known story, "The Ballroom of Romance," with Bridie pulling up the scotch grass that grows among her father's marigolds, and the dance-hall standing by the roadside "with treeless boglands all around and a gravel expanse in front of it," is a merciless piece of recollection of a miserable time in Ireland's history.

Mary Robinson "The Singers," a poem for the heroic women who endured the "unforgiving coast" and harsh life in the West. "Outside History" concerns a greater landscape where stars yet keep their distance, but mortality is an untimely reality.

In "Going Home to Mayo, Winter 1949," Paul Durcan, exiled in "the alien foreign city of Dublin," is driven as a child towards the place of his forebears in Mayo. "Daddy, Daddy," I cried, "Pass out the moon." Like other poets he turns names into verse—those towns through which his father's old Ford Anglia passes: Kilcock, Kinnegad, Strokestown, Elphin, Tarmonbarry, Tulsk, Ballaghaderreen, Ballavarry. . . . Mayo is in Durcan's blood, when as a fourteen-year-old boy in "Backside to the Wind" he walks alone "by the scimitar shores of Killala Bay" dreaming of a French Ireland and "a staple diet of potatoes and wine."

Poet Nuala Ní Dhomhnaill, writing in fluid Irish, also reflects on rural small town life, and the sometimes painful transition between city and country. "Tiomáinim an chairt ar dalladh trí bailte beaga lár na hEireann." (I drive the car like a blind person through the small midland towns.) For her too, the Irish place-names swept through in "An Rás" (The Race) form part of the poetry— "Aonach, Ros Cré, Móinteach Milic" (Nenagh, Roscrea, Mountmellick). Medbh McGuckian's "To a Cuckoo at Coolanlough," beginning with the remarkable image "Driving the perfect length of Ireland,/Like a worn fold in a newspaper," finishes by underlining the possible relationship between landscape and words with the question

And I wonder, after the three minute
News, if you remember
The bits of road that I do?

Eavan Boland's "Anna Liffey" celebrates the river Liffey, its source, its flowing journey, and the capital city where it reaches the sea with a compelling dignity. She feels that the spirit of the water reflects the spirit and history of the place, and of the people. However, Boland also ventures beyond the pale to capture superbly the feeling of Ireland's western landscapes. She dedicated to

County Mayo

County Galway

Cleggan and the nearby coast off Galway has been made poet's territory by Richard Murphy, celebrating Omey Island, and High Island and the seals that live in its caves ("the calamity of seals begins with jaws"). From Cleggan, Murphy wrote a great ballad mourning the Cleggan Disaster, highlighting storm and tragedy. In "My Dark Fathers" Brendan Kennelly, "come of Kerry clay and rock," contemplated the tragic past and famine blight in Munster.

Recent human misery was recorded by Michael Hartnett, "All the perversions of the soul, I learnt on a small farm." "The Small Farm" is a supplement to Kavanagh's "Epic" in Monaghan where neighbors fought "surrounded by our pitchfork-armed claims." John Montague also saw the epic qualities of his place: the Clogher valley where Garvaghy, the Rough Field, lies near Ballygawley, County Tyrone. In "Like Dolmens Round My Childhood, the Old

People," he remembers Mary Moore in her bag-apron and boots, tramping the fields, and living in a crumbling gatehouse "famous as Pisa." The others who haunted him, Jamie MacCrystal, Maggie Owens surrounded by animals and the rest, he exorcises in a beautiful image:

> *For years they trespassed on my dreams*
> *Until once, in a standing circle of stones*

> *I felt their shadows pass*
> *Into that dark permanence of ancient forms.*

In "The Glens" John Hewitt wrote with affection of his own place around Cushendall in County Antrim:

> *Groined by deep glens and walled along the west*
> *By the bare hilltops and the tufted moss*
> *This ruin of arable that ends in foam.*

Field work, West Cork

$\mathcal{S}$eamus Heaney was reared west of the Bann in Derry, in the country around Anahorish, the "place of clear water." Later he wrote of Glanmore, County Wicklow, winter rain dripping among the alders and birch trees, the sounds of the cuckoo and the corncrake consorting in a May twilight. But perhaps many will recall more clearly his boyhood on a Derry farm. Like Yeats saddled with his "Lake Isle of Inisfree," Heaney is in some danger for being better remembered for his poetry of early memory rather than the grandeur of his later themes. The poems of his boyhood life describe the thatcher, the seed cutters chopping the seed potatoes, the Presbyterian neighbor whose head was like a white-washed kitchen hung with texts, the adventures with frogspawn and blackberry picking, and the frosty Christmas Eve where another Protestant neighbor creates a toy battleship. Wells, buckets and windlasses, the smell of waterweed and moss observed as a child are turned into a literary metaphor in "Personal Helicon."

Heaney remembers his father working with a horse-plough or a spade "by God, the old man could handle a spade. Just like his old man." The son declares that he chooses to dig with "the squat pen." His grandfather "cut more turf in a day/Than any other man on Toner's bog." Heaney would reclaim the bog for poetry, a place traditionally avoided by writers—except to evoke fear.

The night is cold on the Great Bog.
The storm is lashing—no small matter

wrote an eighth-century poet. For Heaney "the bogholes might be Atlantic seepage. The wet centre is bottomless." The bog is a place of concealment—it not only hides "the waterlogged trunks of great firs, soft as pulp," butter, and the Great Irish Elk, "an astounding crate full of air," but also the bodies of men and women who perished in ancient rituals. Grauballe Man lies on a Danish pillow of turf "as if he had been poured in tar," the young girl found smothered beneath the turf, centuries before her "betraying sisters" were punished in the Troubles, suffered "the exact and tribal, intimate revenge." The bog continues to be a place of terror.

Bog, County Mayo

Sally Gap, County Wicklow

Derry, Wicklow, and Station Island, the penitential location on Lough Derg in County Donegal, provide landscape for Heaney's contemplation and philosophy. Other contemporary poets with him continue to map Ireland in poetry. Thomas Kinsella, Derek Mahon, Bernard O'Donohue in north Cork, Michael Coady in Tipperary and the rest—their poems of landscape amass like a cairn (the simile is Heaney's).

Those that write in English have sidestepped the dilemma that lies at the core of Brian Friel's play, *Translations*. Friel's theme is the usurpation of language by the conqueror, which he sees as an act of vandalism and pillage. The play is set in 1833 during the lifetime of the Ordnance Survey of Ireland which lasted for a decade. Those who carried out its work were instructed to list details of natural topography, hills, bogs, wood, climate, and ancient landmarks such as ruined churches and graveyards. They were to note details of social economy, road widths, make subjective appreciations of scenery, condemn shebeens and write how women squandered money on tea, while men drank whiskey.

Friel sees the Survey, which did its work a decade before the Famine, as a destructive influence imposed by imperialism. Prosaic English choices are substitutes for beautiful Irish place-names. The sappers who measure and capture the landscape are aided by the stooge, Owen, the translator, who plays a vital part in this unnaming.

Owen: We are trying to denominate and at the same time describe that tiny area of soggy, rocky, sandy ground where that little stream enters the sea, an area known locally as Bun na hAbhann . . . Burnfoot! What about Burnfoot?

Friel spins loyalties and history with tradition and language—place-names are used as a go-between in the love scene between Maire and Lieutenant Yolland; they are desecrated when the list of evictions is announced.

It could be argued that he is not only hard on the Ordnance Survey but also inaccurate, and that the work during one brief decade before it ran out of money was far from destructive. During that period the Survey employed the great Irish scholars Eugene O'Curry, and John O'Donovan whose lifetime's work in Gaelic studies included his treatment of the *Annals of the Four Masters*, a landmark in Irish scholarship. While he was with the Survey, O'Donovan visited every parish in Ireland to learn the correct Irish place-names. O'Donovan, like Friel's character, must have pondered on " . . . a rich language . . . full of mythologies of fantasy and hope and self-deception . . . our response to mud-cabins and a diet of potatoes . . . " But his achievement was immeasurably influential in promoting the preservation of Irish as a spoken language.

Friel's theme of dislocated language and lost hope makes good politics and moving theater. The conflict between Irish and English may continue to be a subject for lamentation as it was when the old poets mourned the passing of Gaelic society. One of the most recent, who has struggled with choice and "the celebrated Anglo-Irish stew," is Michael Hartnett in his *Farewell to English*. But the latest news is that Hartnett has returned to the language of Shakespeare.

Irish or English, the literary landscape widens and the literary cairn continues to rise. Friel has his place there with his continuing celebration of Ballybeg, located firmly in the Donegal countryside, not least in his luminous *Dancing at Lughnasa*, a lament for a beautiful but arid past, more poetically rendered than William Trevor's grim memories.

County Donegal

In general the prominence of landscape in Irish literature has been cause for celebration. One of Amergin's songs written in the ninth century (in Latin, to further muddy the waters of the language controversy) evokes the ideal landscape. It seems that Amergin is singing somewhere near the Kenmare estuary when he calls out in Thomas Kinsella's lovely translation:

> *I call the land of Ireland*
> *much travelled fertile ocean*
> *fertile fruitful mountains,*
> *fruitful showery woods*
> *falls showering in rivers*
> *falls of deep-pooled lakes . . .*
> *I call the land of Ireland.*

Connemara

Biographies

Samuel Beckett (1906–1989), one of Ireland's greatest dramatists, was born in Dublin. In 1937 he moved to Paris where he is buried. His numerous experimental works include plays *Waiting for Godot* (1952), *All that Fall* (1956), *Endgame* (1957), *Happy Days* (1961), *Eh Joe* (1965), *Not I* (1972), *Rockaby* (1981), a volume of short stories *More Pricks than Kicks* (1934), and novels *Murphy* (1938), *Malone Dies* (1951), and *Molloy* (1951). He won the Nobel Prize in Literature in 1969.

Brendan Behan (1923–1964) was in jail in England for IRA activities during 1938–1941. He also spent five years in Mountjoy jail, Dublin, in the early 1940s. His works include plays *The Quare Fellow*, first performed in 1954, and *The Hostage* (1958), and his autobiography *Borstal Boy* (1958). Excessive drinking damaged his health.

Eavan Boland (1944–) was born in Dublin. Her poetry volumes include *New Territory* (1967), *The War Horse* (1975), *In Her Own Image* (1980), *Night Feed* (1982), *The Journey* (1987), *Outside History* (1990), and *In a Time of Violence* (1994).

Elizabeth Bowen (1899–1973) from north Cork wrote numerous short stories, including "Look at all Those Roses" (1941) and "A Day in the Dark" (1965). Her novels include *The Hotel* (1927), *The Last September* (1929), *The House in Paris* (1935), and *The Heat of the Day* (1949). In *Bowen's Court* (1942), she tells of her family and her home.

Jeremiah J. Callanan (1795–1829) was born in Cork. He collected and translated Irish legends and ballads. Among his works is *The Recluse of Inchidoney and Other Poems* (1830). *The Poems of J. J. Callanan* was published in 1847.

Giraldus Cambrensis (1144–1220) visited Ireland as secretary to Prince John in 1184 and wrote two books about the country: *The Conquest of Ireland* (1169) and *The Topography and History of Ireland* (1188). He coined a well-known phrase, criticizing the Norman invaders of 1172 for becoming "more Irish than the Irish themselves." He set a stereotypical and prejudiced view of Ireland for future writers.

Thomas Carlyle (1795–1881) was a Scottish essayist, historian and moralist. His writing includes *Sartor Resartus* (1836), *French Revolution* (1837), *Oliver Cromwell* (1845), and *Reminiscences* (1881).

Michael Coady (1939–) was born in Carrick-on-Suir, Co. Tipperary. A teacher, musician and writer, his poetry reflects the detail of everyday local life. His collections include *Two for a Woman, Three for a Man* (1980) and *Oven Lane* (1987).

Eric Cross (1905–1980), scientist and philosopher, was born in Newry, Co. Down. He wrote *The Tailor and Anstey*, (1942) and *Silence is Golden and Other Stories* (1978).

Thomas Davis (1814–1845) from Mallow, Co. Cork, was a lawyer and political activist, a journalist and poet. In 1842 he, Charles Gavin Duffy and John Blake Dillon founded *The Nation* newspaper. He wrote the poem "Lament for the Death of Eoghan Rua O'Neill" and the words to the song "A Nation Once Again." *The Poems of Thomas Davis* was published in 1846.

Lord Edward Dunsany (1878–1957) was born in London but lived in Co. Meath. A dramatist, short story writer and novelist, his novels include *The Gods of Pegana* (1905), *Time and the Gods* (1906), *The Sword of Wellaran* (1908), *The King of Efland's Daughter* (1924), plays *The Glittering Gate* (1909) and *If* (1921), and poetry. His autobiography is *Patches of Sunlight* (1938).

Paul Durcan (1944–) was born in Dublin. His books of poetry include *O Westport in the Light of Asia Minor* (1975), *Teresa's Bar* (1976), *Jesus, Break His Fall* (1980), *The Berlin Wall Café* (1985) *Going Home to Russia* (1987), *Daddy, Daddy* (1990), *A Snail in My Prime* (1993), and *Christmas Day* (1996).

Maria Edgeworth (1767–1849) was born in England but grew up in Edgeworthstown, Co. Longford. Her first book, *Letters to Literary Ladies*, was published in 1795. She and her father wrote *Practical Education* (1798). She was one of the founders of the realistic novel genre. Her novels include *Castle Rackrent* (1800), *The Absentee* (1812), and *Helen* (1834).

Robin Flower (1881–1946) was a Celtic scholar, translator and poet. He was born in England, educated in Oxford, and worked in the British Museum. He spent much time on the Great Blasket off Co. Kerry, and *The Western Island* is his reminiscence of life on the island. He also wrote *The Irish Tradition* (1947) and several translations, including O'Criomhthain's *The Island Man*.

Brian Friel (1929–), Ireland's best-known contemporary dramatist, is from Co. Donegal. His many plays include *Philadelphia, Here I Come!* (1965), *Lovers* (1968), *The Freedom of the City* (1973), *Volunteers* (1975), *Aristocrats* (1979), *Faith Healer* (1980), *Translations* (1981), *Making History* (1988), *Dancing at Lughnasa* (1990), and *Wonderful Tennessee* (1993).

Oliver Goldsmith (1728–1774) was from Pallas, Co. Longford, and educated at Trinity College, Dublin. He wrote novels including *The Vicar of Wakefield* (1766), poetry, *The Traveller* (1764) and *The Deserted Village* (1770), and the play *She Stoops to Conquer* (1773).

Lady Augusta Gregory (1852–1932) was born in Roxborough, Co. Galway. She married into Coole Park. She, W. B. Yeats and Edward Martyn organized the Irish Literary Theatre. She wrote over thirty plays, including *Gods and Fighting Men* (1904) and *The Rising of the Moon* (1907). Her *Journals* were published in 1946.

Michael Hartnett (1941–) was born in Co. Limerick and lives in Dublin. His poetry collections include *A Farewell to English* (1975, 1978), *Adharca Broic* (1978), *Collected Poems I* (1984), *O'Bruadair* (1985), *Collected Poems II* (1986), *A Necklace of Wrens* (1987) and *Poems to Younger Women* (1988).

Seamus Heaney (1939–), Ireland's best-known contemporary poet and 1996 Nobel Prize winner, was born in Derry. His books of poetry include *Death of a Naturalist* (1966), *Door into the Dark* (1969), *Wintering Out* (1972), *North* (1975), *Field Work* (1979), *Station Island* (1984), *The Haw Lantern* (1987), *Seeing Things* (1991), *Sweeney's Flight* (1992), and *The Spirit Level* (1996). His prose includes *Preoccupations* (1980), *The Government of the Tongue* (1988), *The Place of Writing* (1990) and *The Redress of Poetry* (1995).

John Hewitt (1907–1987) was born in Belfast. He worked in Belfast Museum and Art Gallery before moving to Coventry for a number of years. His poetry volumes include *Conacre* (1943), *Those Swans Remember* (1956), *Out of My Time* (1974), *Mosaic* (1981), and *Loose Ends* (1983).

Frederick Robert Higgins (1896–1941) was born in Foxford, Co. Mayo, but grew up in Co. Meath. He was very interested in Irish folk tradition. His books of poetry include *Island Blood* (1925), *The Dark Breed* (1927), and *Arable Holdings* (1933).

Douglas Hyde (1860–1949) was born in Frenchpark, Co. Roscommon. He devoted his life to the restoration of Irish language and folklore. He became the first president of the Gaelic League and was first president of Ireland (1936–1945). His writing includes *Love Songs of Connaught* (1894), *A Literary History of Ireland* (1899), *The Bursting of the Bubble and Other Irish Plays* (1905), and many verse translations.

James Joyce (1882–1941), one of Ireland's greatest writers, was born in Dublin and died in Zurich, Switzerland. His innovative works include *Dubliners* (1914), *A Portrait of the Artist as a Young Man* (1916), *Ulysses* (1922), and *Finnegan's Wake* (1939).

Patrick Kavanagh (1904–1967) was from Co. Monaghan but moved to Dublin. A poet, perhaps the most famous of his works is *The Great Hunger* (1942). He also wrote novels, including *Tarry Flynn* (1948). His autobiography, *The Green Fool*, was published in 1938.

John B. Keane (1928–199_) has written plays, including *Sive* (1959), *The Year of the Hiker* (1964), *The Field* (1965), and *Big Maggie* (1969), short stories, letters, and novels, including *The Bodhrán Maker* (1986) and *Durango* (1991).

Molly Keane (1905–1995), formerly writing as M. J. Farrell, lived in Co. Waterford. Her novels include *Devoted Ladies* (1934), *Two Days in Aragon* (1941), *Treasure Hunt* (1952), *Good Behaviour* (1981), *Time After Time* (1983), and *Loving and Giving* (1988).

Brendan Kennelly (1936–) was born in Co. Kerry. He is a Professor of English at Trinity College, Dublin. His volumes of poetry include *My Dark Fathers* (1964), *Getting Up Early* (1966), *Dream of a Black Fox* (1968), *Bread* (1971), *A Kind of Trust* (1975), *Islandman* (1977), *The Boats Are Home* (1980), *Cromwell* (1983), *The Book of Judas* (1991), and *Poetry My Arse* (1995).

Thomas Kinsella (1928–) was born in Dublin and was professor of English at Temple University, Philadelphia, for twenty years. His books of poetry include *Another September* (1958), *Downstream* (1962), *Nightwalker and Other Poems* (1968) *Peppercanister Poems 1972–1978* (1980), *Songs of the Psyche* (1985), *Out of Ireland* (1987), *Blood and Family* (1988), *Personal Places* (1990), and *From Centre City* (1994). He translated *The Táin* (1969) and *An Duanaire: Poems of the Dispossessed 1600–1900* (1981).

Mary Lavin (1912–1996) was born of Irish parents in Massachusetts. She moved to Ireland at the age of ten, living in Co. Galway and later in Dublin. She wrote nineteen collections of short stories, the first being *Tales from Bective Bridge* (1942), with an introduction by Lord Dunsany, which won the James Tait Black Memorial Prize.

Emily Lawless (1845–1913) was a novelist and poet born at Lyons Castle, Co. Kildare, the daughter of Lord Cloncurry. Her novels include *Hurrish* (1886), *With Essex in Ireland* (1890), and *Grania* (1892).

Francis Ledwidge (1891–1917) was born in Slane, Co. Kildare, and was active in the Gaelic League. He wrote a number of nature poems, and Lord Dunsany had his first collection, *Songs of the Field* (1915), published. Dunsany edited Ledwidge's *Complete Poems* in 1919, two years after Ledwidge was killed in WWI.

Sheridan Le Fanu (1814–1873) was born in Dublin where he received his university education. He was a successful journalist and fiction writer, but stopped due to political and family problems. He resumed fiction-writing later in life, and his books include *The House by the Churchyard* (1861–1863), *Uncle Silas* (1864), *Checkmate* (1871), *Chronicles of Golden Friars* (1871), and *In a Glass Darkly* (1872).

John McGahern (1934–) was born in Dublin. His novels include *The Barracks* (1962), *The Dark* (1965), *Nightlines* (1970), *The Leavetaking* (1975), *The Pornographer* (1979), *High Ground* (1985), *Amongst Women* (1990), and *The Power of Darkness* (1991).

Medbh McGuckian (1950–) was born in Belfast. Her poetry collections include *The Flower Master* (1982), *Venus and the Rain* (1984), *On Ballycastle Beach* (1988), *Marconi's Cottage* (1991), and *The Lavendar Hat* (1994).

Bryan MacMahon (1909–) from Listowel, Co. Kerry, now a retired school principal, has written collections of short stories including *The Lion Tamer*, *The Tallystick* (1994), and *The Sound of Hooves*, a novel *The Honeyspike* (1967), and his memoir, *The Master* (1992). He translated *Peig* by Peig Sayers.

Louis MacNeice (1907–1963) was born in Belfast and educated in Oxford. His writing includes the critical work *Modern Poetry* (1938), and books of verse *Blind Fireworks* (1929), *Autumn Journal* (1939), *Springboard* (1944), *Ten Burnt Offerings* (1952), and *Visitations* (1959). He wrote a play, *Out of the Picture* (1937).

Derek Mahon (1941–) was born in Belfast. He has published several books of poetry including *Night Crossing* (1968), *Lives* (1972), *The Snow Party* (1975), *Courtyards in Delft* (1981), *The Hunt by Night* (1982), *Antartica* (1986), and edited with Peter Fallon *The Penguin Book of Contemporary Irish Poetry* (1990). Mahon lives in New York.

James Clarence Mangan (1803–1849), political activist, translator and poet, was born in Dublin. He wrote articles and poetry for various magazines and journals. Writing in the mid 1800s, the Irish Famine and the Young Irelanders had a profound effect upon his work. He supported John Mitchel's call to the United Irishmen for a violent approach. He is most famous for his ballad "Dark Rosaleen," and poems "A Vision of Connaught in the Thirteenth Century" and "Siberia."

Charles Robert Maturin (1782–1824) was born in Dublin and educated at Trinity College. His romantic novels include *Melmoth the Wanderer* (1820).

Rev. William Hamilton Maxwell (1794–1850) was born in Newry, Co. Down, and educated at Trinity College, Dublin. He was fascinated by military life. His novels include *O'Hara* (1825), and *The Dark Lady of Doona* (1836). *Wild Sports of the West* (1832) is his best-known work.

Brian Merriman (1749–1805) was a Co. Clare schoolmaster in the late 1700s. He is famous for his long dream poem (aisling) *The Midnight Court* (1780).

John Montague (1929–) was born in Brooklyn, New York, and raised in Co. Tyrone. His poetry collections include *Poisoned Lands* (1961, 1977), *A Chosen Light* (1967), *Tides* (1970), *The Rough Field* (1972), *A Slow Dance* (1975), *The Great Cloak* (1978), *The Dead Kingdom* (1984), and *Mount Eagle* (1988). His fiction includes *Death of a Chieftain* (1967) and *The Lost Notebook* (1987).

Lady Sydney Morgan (1776–1859) was educated in Dublin. She published *Twelve Original Hibernian Melodies* (1805). Her novels include *The Wild Irish Girl* (1806), *O'Donnel* (1814), and *Florence Macarthy* (1818). Her nonfiction work includes *Italy* (1821), which was commended, and *The Life and Times of Salvator Rosa* (1824).

George Moore (1852–1933) was a landowner in Co. Mayo. He studied in London, and lived in Paris for seven years. His writing includes novels, *A Drama in Muslin* (1886), *The Lake*, and *Esther Waters* (1894), his autobiography, *Hail and Farewell* (1911–1914), political sketches and essays, *Parnell and his Island* (1887), and a collection of short stories, *The Untilled Field* (1903).

Fynes Moryson visited Ireland and, influenced by Giraldus Cambrensis, wrote his *Itinerary* (1617) which implied the Irish were an uncivilized race.

Richard Murphy (1927–) was born in the west of Ireland. His poetry collections include *Sailing to an Island* (1963), *The Battle of Aughrim* (1968), *High Island* (1974), *The Price of Stone* (1985), and *The Mirror Wall* (1989). He lives in Dublin.

Nuala Ní Dhomhnaill (1952–) was born in Lancashire and grew up in the Kerry Gaeltacht. She has lived in Holland and Turkey. Her collections of poems in Irish include *An Dealg Droighin* (1981), *Féar Suaithinseach* (1984), and *Feis* (1991). *Pharaoh's Daughter* (1991), and *The Astrakhan Cloak* (1991) were published with English translations.

Edna O'Brien (1930–) was born in Co. Clare and lives in London. She has written a number of novels, including *The Country Girls* (1960), *Girl With Green Eyes* (1962), *August Is a Wicked Month* (1965), *I Hardly Knew You* (1977), and

The House of Splendid Isolation (1994).

Flann O'Brien (1911–1966) was born in Strabane, Co. Tyrone, but moved to Dublin where he was educated at UCD. A journalist and satirist, sometimes under the name of Myles na Gopeleen, his writing includes *The Third Policeman* (written in 1940), *At-Swim-Two-Birds* (1939), *An Béal Bocht* (1941), *The Hard Life* (1961), and *The Dalkey Archive* (1964). His real name was Brian O'Nolan.

Sean O'Casey (1880–1964) was born in Dublin. He was secretary of the Irish Citizen Army and a founder member of the Irish Labour Party. His plays include *The Shadow of a Gunman* (1923), *Juno and the Paycock* (1924), *The Plough and the Stars* (1926), *The Silver Tassie* (1928) and *Red Roses for Me* (1942). The first volume of his six-part autobiography is *I Knock at the Door* (1939).

Frank O'Connor (1903–1966) was born in Cork, and worked as a librarian. He wrote many collections of short stories including *Guests of the Nation*. *An Only Child* (1961) is his autobiography.

Tomás O'Criomhthain (1856–1937) was born on the Great Blasket, off the Kerry coast. He wrote an account of his life in *An t-Oileánach* (*The Islandman*) (1929), and a journal of island impressions, *Allagar na hInise* (1928). *Seanchas a hIniseournal* (*Lore from the Western Island*) (1956) was compiled from his storytelling by Robin Flower.

Eugene O'Curry (1796–1862) was born in Co. Clare. He wrote poetry in favor of Catholic Emancipation. In 1835 he was appointed to the Topographical Section of the Ordnance Survey, working with George Petrie, the director. With John O'Donovan he edited a volume *Ancient Laws of Ireland*. In 1854, he became Professor of Irish History and Archaeology at the Catholic University. He also collected Irish music.

Máirtín O'Direáin (1910–1988) was born on Inishmore, the largest of the Aran Islands. While working in Galway, he became involved in Irish language theater. He moved to the Civil Service in Dublin in 1938. His collections of poetry include *Coinnle Geala* (1942), *Dánta Aniar* (1943), *Rogha Dánta* (1949) *O Morna agus Dánta Eile* (1957), and *Ar Ré Dheard D* (1963). He received awards for his work.

John O'Donovan (1806–1861) was born in Co. Kilkenny. He worked for the Irish Record Office in 1826 and became the Irish language adviser to the Ordnance Survey. During 1834–41, he travelled all over Ireland, collecting details on all aspects of topography, language and folklore. He worked on the *Annals of the Four Masters*, and on *Ancient Laws of Ireland*.

Seán O'Faoláin (1910–1991) was born in Cork. He founded the monthly journal *The Bell*. A political activist, he wrote many short stories including "The Patriot" and "The Silence of the Valley." Collections include *Midsummer Night Madness* (1932) and *The Heat of the Sun* (1966). Novels include *Bird Alone* (1936). *Vive Moi!* (1964) is his autobiography.

Liam O'Flaherty (1896–1984) was born on Inishmore, in the Aran Islands. His writing includes novels, *Thy Neighbour's Wife* (1924), *The Informer* (1925), *The Assassin* (1928), *Skerrett* (1932), *Famine* (1937), *Insurrection* (1950), and collections of short stories.

Fr. Eugene O'Growney (1863–1899) was an Irish language revivalist. He became Professor of Celtic Literature and Language at the university in Maynooth, and Vice-President of the Gaelic League. He emigrated to America for health reasons. He wrote numerous articles for Irish magazines and paper, and his *Simple Lessons in Irish* (1894) proved very popular.

Muiris O'Súilleabháin (1904–1950) was born on the Great Blasket, off the Kerry coast. He joined the Gardaí Siochána (police force) in Connemara, where he lived until his tragic death by drowning in Galway. His autobiography *Fiche Blian ag Fás* (*Twenty Years a-Growing*) (1933) offers an insight into life on the Blasket Islands.

Seamus O'Sullivan (1879–1958) was a poet, essayist and editor, born in Dublin. *Twilight People* was his first book of poetry. *The Earth-Lover* (1909) provides an insight into Dublin life. He edited *The Dublin Magazine*.

Thomas William Rolleston (1857–1920) was a translator and poet from Co. Offaly. He was founding editor of the *Dublin University Review* in 1885, and was Secretary of the Irish Literary Society in London in 1892. His work includes *Sea Spray: Verses and Translations* (1909) which contains his "The Dead at Clonmacnois."

Peig Sayers (1873–1958), from Dunquin, Co. Kerry, worked in Dingle before she married on to the Blasket Islands. Entitled Queen of the Storytellers, she wrote *Peig* (1936) and *Machtnamh Sean Mhná* (*An Old Woman's Reflections*) (1939).

Somerville & Ross: Violet Martin (1862–1915), from Ross House, Galway, wrote under the name Martin Ross. In 1886, she met her second cousin **Edith Somerville** (1858–1949), from Drishane House, Castletownsend, Co. Cork. They formed the successful writing duo of Somerville & Ross and published five novels: *An Irish Cousin* (1889), *Naboth's Vineyard* (1891), *The Real Charlotte* (1894), *The Silver Fox* (1898), and *Dan Russel the Fox* (1911), as well as three volumes of the *Irish R.M.* series. Somerville continued to write after Martin's death.

Edmund Spenser (1552–1599) was born in London and came to Ireland in 1580 as secretary to the new lord deputy, Lord Grey. He then moved to north Cork where he was granted a 3,000-acre estate under Queen Elizabeth's resettlement scheme of 1587. His writing includes The Shepheardes Calender (1579), *The Faerie Queene*, *Colin Clout's Come Home Again* (1595), and *A View of the Present State of Ireland*.

Bram Stoker (1847–1912) was born in Dublin and educated in Trinity College. He wrote the horror classic about the vampire *Dracula* (1897). Other books include *The Mystery of the Sea* (1902) and *Famous Imposters* (1910).

Jonathan Swift (1667–1745) was educated in Kilkenny and Trinity College, Dublin. He returned to Dublin in 1714 as Dean of St. Patrick's Cathedral. He provided satire and commentary on issues of the time in his *Drapier's Letters* (1724–1725) and "A Modest Proposal." He also wrote the classic tale *Gulliver's Travels* (1726).

John Millington Synge (1871–1909) visited the Aran Islands for the first time in 1898 whence he drew much of his inspiration. A director of Dublin's Abbey Theatre, he wrote *In the Shadow of the Glen* (1903), *Riders to the Sea* (1904), *The Tinker's Wedding* (1908), *The Well of the Saints* (1905), *The Playboy of the Western World* (1907), the unfinished *Deirdre of the Sorrows* (1910), as well as poems and translations.

William Trevor (1928–) from Co. Cork was educated in Dublin. He has won several writing awards. His writing includes radio and television plays, short stories, and novels including *A Standard of Behaviour* (1956), *The Old Boys* (1964), *The Ballroom of Romance* (1972), *Angels at the Ritz* (1975), *Lovers of Their Time* (1978), *Beyond the Pale* (1981), *Fools of Fortune* (1983), *Two Lives* (1991), and *Felicia's Journey* (1994).

Anthony Trollope (1815–1882) was born in London. He moved to Ireland in 1841 as a postal surveyor and traveled the country, using this experience in his early writing. His forty-seven novels include *The Warden* (1855), first of the six chronicles of Darsetshire, and *Can You Forgive Her?* (1864), first of the six in the Palliser series.

W. B. Yeats (1865–1939), one of Ireland's greatest poets, was born in Dublin, educated in London and Dublin, and spent many summers in Co. Sligo. His several collections of poetry include *Crossways* (1889), *The Rose* (1893), *The Wind Among the Reeds* (1899), *In the Seven Woods* (1904), *The Green Helmet and Other Poems* (1910), *Responsibilities* (1914), *The Wild Swans at Coole* (1919), *Michael Robartes and the Dancer* (1921), *The Tower* (1928), *The Winding Stair and Other Poems* (1933), and *Last Poems* (1936–1939).